HEAD GIRL

HEAD GIRL

Freya Daly Sadgrove

Victoria University of Wellington Press

VICTORIA UNIVERSITY OF
WELLINGTON
TE HERENGA WAKA

Victoria University of Wellington Press
PO Box 600, Wellington
New Zealand
vup.wgtn.ac.nz

A catalogue record is available at the National Library of New Zealand

ISBN 9781776562961

Published with the assistance of a grant from

ARTS COUNCIL OF NEW ZEALAND *TOI AOTEAROA*

Printed in Singapore by Markono Print Media Pte Ltd

for my enemies

CONTENTS

3

HUMAN EVOLUTION

I am curled up
in the vast body of my dread like the daughter
of a pestilential insect :
a larva   calmly knitting itself an existence—
an evil thing , and soft—   revolving in the dark

I am angry   no   no I am not :
I am asleep and dreaming of anger   I am asleep

I am developing armour made of minuscule teeth
in ten years I will be ready to fight

1

HOUSE RULES

you can't give me a kiss while Joy Division is playing ..... and tell me you'll tear ..... me ..... apart ..... and then unfollow me on Instagram .... you can't keep doing hot things like ..... blinking .... you can't invite me over and introduce me to your damn hens ..... if they are not all named after me .... you can't seduce me upon my return from hospital .... you can't play a jaunty tune on your pan pipes when I am trying to masturbate .... you can't go around not telling everyone you see ..... including strangers ..... about me .... you can't bounce on a trampoline ..... with a torch jammed in your crotch ..... and call out to me *does yours glow like mine* .... you can't jump out of a hedge in front of me ..... on a country road ..... and not have me fall in love with you .... you can't remember my name .... you can't stamp on my face ..... even though it is right there .... do not give me food or a ride in your car .... you can't introduce me to your friend ..... and have them compliment my smile with a resigned look .... you can't change my life .... you can't take my arm in yours and take me home via a glow worm cave ..... that is just not right .... you can't trivialise my psychiatric condition ..... oh wait ..... yeah you can .... you can't make me feel special for more than twenty-four hours or you'll trigger the alarm .... in this house we know that to drive away a boy ..... is effortless

I USED TO BE HEAD GIRL OF MY HIGH SCHOOL
AND NOW I AM A MASSIVE CUNT

my high school boyfriend told me about his depression   on a berm

the berm was in Karori where 35 percent of berms are
I burst into tears   with real human efficiency
and then I got depression too   out of empathy   or fomo
I got asthma the same way   when I was five years old
kicking the back of the passenger seat :   *me too actually   I have that too*

I started taking lithium because some lady wrote about it on the internet
and it sounded cool   but then lithium made me fat
I totally wouldn't care   except   my boobs have started oozing
over the top of my bra like fart putty with two fingers in it
and I cannot afford a new bra

look I can't help being a go-getter
if life shoves a walnut through your ribs   it's your destiny
to go get more walnuts   it's the story of my success
just take a look at me now
now I have ten to twelve walnuts in and around me
cleverly disguised as corks on a traditional Australian outback hat
but actually taking up a lot of my field of vision

in each of them I have carved one little word :   *cunt*
and I go around   I just go around   I just go around and around
and they are whirring in my face but I don't let it get me down
I'm just going around and around
wearing a pink dress and laughing directly to camera

IN SHREK WHEN FIONA SAYS ' THIS IS NOT DIGNIFIED ! '

   I remember taking a shit once in Year One
and my two best friends demanded to come look at it afterwards
   ' disgusting ! ' they remarked
   I was embarrassed   but also pleased

   I have carpet burn on my knees
which I hate now that I am finally a woman
   I hate the way I look up at boys.....   I say
to my friends at a cool sleepover   wiggling my brows
   they are impressed   I can tell

   every time I try to wink I go cross-eyed
which is a difficult thing to build your sexuality around
but everyone loves and appreciates it like   thin ham—
that thin Italian ham
   but my fingernails   ha
no one loves and appreciates my fingernails
and my rumpus room is   filled with old meat
and my breath.....   my breath comes in and out of my mouth

   but I got tactics like : yeah easy
   you just shove a tube   down the throat of any silence
and shout right into it   it's a cool way to chat
   and you can dance   in someone's lap

   ugh can you just humour me though   I have like , bad self-esteem
so I really need you all   balls deep in love with ya girl

o fate   you inhumane bastard—
stick my face in the heat of the moment and rub it around
like a dog in piss
so I can never lean in for the kiss
    allow me instead to climb into my steamroller
and drive it slowly over the elastic blister   of my feminine power—
make it burst   and shower lymph on the gathering crowds

YOU BETTER JERK BITCH

emotions are sacred to boys :
you mustn't take them in vain

I mean I mustn't say things like :   I love.....
to imagine you   glancing up from our Facebook chat—
smiling at Kate   dropping your phone on a pile of clothes—
peeling off her jeans
I love to imagine you going slowly down on Kate—
making Kate feel really..........unique
I mustn't say that
I mustn't say I really love the way you   glance both ways
before kissing me in the street

I intend to come to your birthday party and
fucking flirt with your cousin—
bend over you at a table—
make you clear your throat like a dumbass teenager
but you won't because   you are just
dripping with self-control

dude I bet you practise magic tricks alone in your room
or I want to bet you practise magic tricks alone in your room
I'd like to see you on your knees
crawling to me   I'd like to see you recognise your error
or at least stop trusting your gut
otherwise we'll never get anywhere

no one else in my life is fascinated by you
but if you are ordinary and you don't even worship me
then I must be mistaken about being a god
and I know I'm not

BAD SEX IN BIG SUBURBS

what will you give up for closeness honey bun

you can get anyone onside   with enough booze
and ruthless gentleness   people are gagging for a little kindness
    people will kill for sympathy   these are the seasons of mists baby
and I'm in business   I'm a life coach
and I say let's get drunk among your family   compose six texts
to your gap-filler crush
and send them off in a volley of triumph   from under the dinner table

    pay for me !!! pay for my soul
I'm long-lasting   god I'm so durable
I'm *honestly stronger than you know*
    I'm like the condom with chemicals in
so you can fuck for ages   but never come

    I'm in a nurse uniform   a sexy nurse uniform
with a chart on a clipboard
    let's work out how much hate you can take
and make sure you take the hate on a daily basis
in big wet dollops on your ragged heart
    ooh   are you sad   why don't you go write a poem about it

    I can tell you're very proud to know   that no girl has ever owned you
    you are your own man   such a fine young man
I have therefore prepared for you a certificate
    I know how you like certificates baby   yeah
you like that marbled cardstock don't you   say it
    look I photocopied my signature especially

ah come on   just tell me you love me the most
out of every single person my age oh my god   I just wanna be all
tell me a secret   so you'll tell me something fake
for the sake of having something to say   ha ha   I sit in mystery like it's bird shit
which is not how you're supposed to do it

hey write me a poem but make it
the kind you'll get embarrassed about in exactly four years
four years is how long it takes the empathy you have for yourself
to deteriorate   yeah and I want exactly that much   um discomfort

twenty-somethings are just deformed teenagers with rent to pay
old people aren't wise they've just got more   context
I'm a guru and I want free money
if I were a boy I would cry at a different bus stop every day

PETTY VIGILANTE

here I come world   here I come   modern life
driving a tempest !   of justice !!!
    there will be no hiding from me
for I am the omnipotent bitch !!!
    I transcend knowledge   just as you would half expect of me—
just as they will say at my funeral :
ah   she transcended knowledge
    what a shame she has died

    yeah well you know who else is gonna die
you are ! all of you—
all my personal baddies—every individual
who has ever made me feel
less like a person than I   ought   to feel
    I don't care if you have   a beautiful singing voice
    I don't care if you volunteer !   for a crisis helpline
    I don't care if you have clout in the industry
    I don't care if you fight climate change—
    if you ever made me feel *bad*
then..........fuck the ice caps !!!!!   let them overflow the ocean
    the world is full of approx. twenty bad girls and boys
and I am coming for you all   like Santa but shitty

    it's so selfish of you to have hurt me specifically
    it makes me want to crush you
    it makes me want to press you down till you can feel it in your past
    I want to press you down till your memories change shape
    I just want to teach you how to hate yourself—
someone has to   cos I can tell you never bothered to learn
and I take exception to that

TEN EARTHQUAKES RIGHT NOW

our bodies are normal but enthusiastic

sex is everywhere   you can't open your eyes
without a bit of sex getting in   for example here in Wellington
beds creak resolutely in all the houses   and the children are so
unworried

I'm such an adult compared to children
I'm such an adult for you   doing my worry for you
by which I mean doing sex   which is so adult   and so worried

a sex thought I have is that
your bones aren't impressive   they're just arranged that way
I refuse to be charmed by you   just
uh   who do you have to screw around here
to make absolutely sure you don't screw anyone else

ha ha   your skin makes me laugh   with my mouth half closed
while I am cataloguing your various soft and hard parts

ha   you think you're made of marble
but you give yourself away when you move

I say it's me   doing very old magic to animate you :
sex golem
I pretend not to know you're pretending   cos I love the way
you play along   it's so uh   hot it's like
this is a kink thing   you're into it

ooh   let's pathologise me :
I'm manic like Planet Earth   I'm depressed like a.....dinner plate

23

it's normal to feel most at home in Briscoes
home is where the homewares are

for nice sex I recommend :
get yourself a girl who can do both   uh   the earthquake
and the fine china

YES MAN GIRL

the last vestiges of my self-respect   of which there are
exactly four   are standing around a well-lit room
dressed as angels   four angels
    they are tutting   just as angels must tut
    there's a butler with a tray of blinis   it's all dignified as hell   it's all
pinky fingers in the air like tiny thin boners

    but now !   me and my feelings are bursting in
and bowling the butler over
    my feelings flank me ; we are quintessential hot teens
    we stomp forwards half smiling   in little shorts with our legs shaved—
we all come to a standstill at the same moment   but it doesn't look planned
    that's talent   pure talent

    the butler composes himself   fetches ice water
    the angels are boomer-aged and they're exchanging looks

    we are here to negotiate   a settlement !
    we are hot-shots brokering our stance on love
    above our little shorts me and my feelings are wearing tailored blazers
with three-quarter sleeves   we are not sweating   we are.....moisturised

    but things go quickly awry in the well-lit room :
our professionalism was a Trojan horse   my feelings are now swarming out
through the butt-flap of our professionalism
    one has pounced on the butler and is peeling off his fake moustache
    another has dropped to a crouch
and her face is turning red and flickering like a time-lapse video of itself—
she is diligently sprouting thick dark hairs all over her body   that is her role—
and another   another is body-slamming a wall
    it is falling over backwards..........to reveal a large film studio

and all the cameras are pointing at—oh my gosh !—me   I feel compelled
to pause and wave   while the crew looks stunned for a moment
and then acts as if nothing has changed   I try to share a knowing look
with the director , but she doesn't engage
    I have to pretend to be chill about this..........I have to focus !
    I have to hiss at my feelings to settle down   I have to rub my temples
and listen to the tiny tiny smackings of angels pursing their lips

        this is the point where I fucken   take my fucken seat
in a shiny black swivel chair at the head of the table
    unfortunately no one else sits
    I am about to express my indignation when   suddenly the room goes dark
    oh   a man has entered and apparently wants to watch his show ?
    he hasn't said anything but we can tell
by the way he has switched off all the lights   and switched on
the big screen at one end of the room
    well everyone stands around in silence   avoiding one another's eyes
for the twenty-three-minute duration of the episode   (it's normal TV
but he can skip the ads   because he is a powerful
middle-aged man)   until he gets up and leaves
    he doesn't turn the lights back on..........
    one of the angels has to sidle over and flick the switch

        ' WE'RE HERE TO TALK ABOUT LOVE !!! '
someone yells out in frustration   in order that we can get back to it
but it is of course me who yelled and therefore no one attends
    I yell that kind of shit all the time
    fortunately I perceive a gavel close at hand—
I bang it on my briefcase and everyone stops murmuring.....
for once in their lives

        one greying member of the order of my self-respect steps forward ,
halo glinting in the strip lighting

' ladies ' she intones
' if we cannot ask for love from others   then.....what can we ask for '
     there is a pause while we all consider her rhetoric
          ' well ' says my dimmest feeling   ' we could ask
to be taken to bone-town—
we could say *take me to bone-town , baby* '
     uh oh.....a chair creaks
and the angel who spoke disappears in a puff of dust
     everyone blinks

(the butler mutters a question   but it is irrelevant)

     the feeling who pushed the wall down
extricates herself now from the passionate embrace
of a film crew production assistant   to join the debate :
' that was premature '
she says of the angel's little detonation
     the production assistant stumbles back among the cameras
wiping their mouth   oh
the feeling looks a lot like my friend Ursula
which is sort of annoying cos I thought
she might look more like me   being   you know
one of my own feelings
and I'd have liked to see my own face get pashed—
I'd obviously be into that
but I guess I'm glad to see Ursula's face cos it's getting out of hand here
     it'd be good if it was really Ursula instead of just the feeling I have
that looks like her

     she puts her hands on her hips and lines up
my three remaining self-respects—
says   ' my bitches   my gals   my special doves..........
you gotta stop disappearing in a puff of dust '

the angels promise to do their darnedest
they squeeze each other's hands

   the feeling who peeled off the butler's moustache
and who is now lingering around him   trying to kiss him inside the ear
like a sexy blowfly   pipes up now :
' don't worry about them—look at me over here—
I have just about got this little man to love me '

   (the butler says ' oh god ')

   my best and biggest feeling   who is dangling heavily from a light fixture
launches herself down now   right through the head of one of the three angels
   pooff!
   we all pause for a second to blink dust out of our eyes
and then there are two   they look fucken scared now
   I think I gotta be the peacekeeper now
   I always gotta keep the peace and it bores me to tears
so I am really crying when I say to my feelings   ' okay now ladies '
   ' .....yeah '
   ' I don't remember ever saying this was a fight to the death '

   the butler starts laughing with his stupid voice
and I think I want to hate him   but the relevant feeling is hiding
under the conference table   scraping plaque off her teeth with a fingernail
and swallowing it

   all my feelings see the butler laughing   so they start laughing too
   everyone is just   losing their shit—
even my two self-respects are starting to titter
   if I'm honest I am beginning to feel   hmm.....
majorly fucked with   but I cover it well   by screaming
and actually pissing myself

the feeling on the butler—she is actually   on the butler now—
clambering around on his back—calls out   ' shut up babycakes ,
you think you're the boss but you're not ,
do what the psychologist says babycakes ,
just sit back and watch '

and she starts slipping the butler's waistcoat off   unbuttoning
his shirt   kissing his neck exactly how you're supposed
to kiss necks

    one angel turns to look me in the eyes now
before she explodes   but the rest of my feelings
barely notice the pitter-patter of little self-respects on their skin
    they are advancing on the butler now too—
stripping slowly   sucking their fingers and slipping them under
the cups of their bras

    I lean back in my chair   I always do what I'm told
    all my feelings are converging now on his butler dick—
even the one who looks like Ursula
    the feeling on the butler's back bites his earlobe
and asks   ' do you love us '

    and now   my last angel is getting up on the table
    she is wonderfully ungainly—
unaccustomed to this kind of showmanship
    she rolls an ankle in her kitten heel and turns pale
and as my feelings start to lap   pleadingly
at the butler's exceptionally ordinary appendage
my last angel explodes with unanticipated exuberance
    many hot sparks land on my skin
but I don't flinch
    my attention is focussed on the butler and my feelings

everyone is naked now   the feeling draped around his shoulders
asks again ,   ' do you love us '
    the butler throws his head back—
he gasps now :   ' no ! '
    ' do you love us ! '
    ' nooooo ! '

    I am coming really hard now   my body goes
all rigid and twisted like..........
petrified chewing gum   in a fossil of a human skull

    ' no ! ' he crows one final time
and manages a money shot for each of my feelings
    wow like.....good for him   I think
as I tumble selflessly off my swivel chair

GEORGIE PORGIE

I wanna kiss you and make you cry   obviously
I find you dangerously unsentimental   in fact I worry
that you might be harbouring a small violence in your daily life
such as   such as muttering insults at the elderly
or writing scathing reviews of high school plays
or like   discreetly growing a tumour   out of revenge

I require you to learn from my softness   otherwise
I will accidentally learn from your hardness   ah
you can't talk about boys and hardness without thinking about   you know
and you have a really nice   you know
but that's not the issue at hand   so to speak   not right now anyway
come to my house later   come   to my house
and I will put your   issue   in my hand

it's not exactly a problem that you don't love me
it's just surprising : look at me   I'm startlingly lovely—
not visually so much as   theoretically
I took a lot of cheap advice and now I love myself too much
it offends the elderly and it bores the young
and you   it does something to you
but you don't like having things done to you   so I stop doing it
I just hover at your bedroom door not doing it

CHAMPAGNE FOR MY REAL FRIENDS , CHAMPAGNE ALSO FOR MY..
..................OTHER FRIENDS

just because someone will probably cry
at your funeral if you die within the next   five years
doesn't mean you can trust them.....   I tell my child in the year 2039
my child is taking notes   my child is taking me seriously
self-care can suck my ass ,   I tell my child
and you better believe it can suck yours too
at the other end of the couch   my child punches the air with a tiny fist

you can't be friends with yourself the way you can be friends
with someone else ;   you can treat yourself but you can't romance yourself ;
you can fuck yourself   but it's not making love

it's 2019 and I have this friend who can go fuck herself
I've got a boner for her feeling lonely
it's 2019 and the air between me and her stings with politeness
and inside the politeness is some very sexy female cruelty
like pass the parcel for assholes
we both try to hold on to it for longer than the other
on other days she cries on my other friends
my sexuality is :   when this happens I want to lean against a wall
and watch

TANTRUM IN A SUPERMARKET

I'm somewhere pathetic when I finally crack
like I'm at Laserforce or I'm patting a stranger's dog
or I've wandered into a vape shop by accident
or I'm in the laundry items aisle

I crack and the crack goes right up through me
it's not exactly ripping myself a new asshole—
it's taking the asshole I've got and making it.....way bigger
so that the wind rushes through me with an unearthly howl
and as it surges outward
through all of humanity
everyone flees
everyone runs to the sea
everyone runs to the sea except me
everyone wades in and drowns   and no one comes back
I spend the rest of my short life   looting canned food and nice clothes
from abandoned shops in the CBD

but in fact !   all of this is untrue..........I've been lying
no one ever left in the first place   and I never even cracked
I never crack because I like it here   I like to play my little games—
I like to tell my little jokes   I like to make   my gentle threats
there are people everywhere and I am always lying to them
like this : *look at me !!!*   *look at me run*   when in fact I am standing still
I haven't moved for several minutes
why does everyone keep believing me
it's not that I'm a baddie I'm just
always wrong

and it's not my fault ! in fact I have a congenital disease of wrongness
I grew up getting severely bested in arguments   I'd be like

losing my mind in the back of the car   my dumb little voice
rising higher and higher   my sister smirking her smirk of righteousness
when I was straining for some kind of point   like you know
exactly like straining for a shit before it is ready
    you can't fucking take it back man   once you've strained enough
    I'd be so embarrassed if it was just my personality   it's so fortunate that I
have my   congenital disease to blame

    oh no I'm lying again   sorry it happens literally all the time
    I wasn't born with it
    I actually developed it as a public service :
I have to cry wolf so the villagers   can get their   satisfaction
    I have to be wrong so that you can be right
    it's actually..........charity   I'm doing charity on you   psych

I DON'T CARE WHO YOU ARE WHERE YOU'RE FROM WHAT YOU DID AS LONG AS YOU LOVE ME

I WANT TO LOVE AND BE LOVED BY THOUSANDS OF MEN I WANT TO BE THE UNYIELDING INDESCRIBABLE OBJECT OF DESIRE I DON'T THINK ENOUGH PEOPLE KNOW HOW BEAUTIFUL I AM NAKED I WAS TRYING TO KEEP TRACK BUT I LOST MY DIARY I LOST IT IN FEBRUARY MUM TOLD ME SHE SOMETIMES WONDERS WHAT SHE DID WRONG WHEN WE WERE LITTLE SHE ALSO PLEADED WITH ME NOT TO INDULGE IN TOO MUCH PROMISCUOUS BEHAVIOUR BUT I IGNORED HER BECAUSE I WISH TO BE WORSHIPPED I WISH TO BE AN INFLUENCE I WISH TO BE IMMORTALISED IN MANY FORMS AND TO WITNESS THE RISE AND FALL OF THOSE FORMS WITHIN MY LIFETIME I WISH TO BE ETERNAL WHILE I AM AWAKE

MAYBE IF YOU'D KNOWN ME WHEN I WAS A TEENAGER I WOULD HAVE MADE YOU SHIFT IN YOUR SEAT THINKING ABOUT MY NEW BODY MY NEW THOUGHTS MY NEW SEX BODY MY SOFT SKIN MY THIN LIMBS PERHAPS YOUR EYELIDS WOULD HAVE FLICKERED IMAGINING THE RUSTLE OF MY UNIFORM SKIRT SUCH HEAVY PRACTICAL FABRIC SUCH AN UNBELIEVABLE EVENT TO FEEL A BOY'S HAND SLIDE UP MY THIGH TO MAKE MY UNSUSPECTING PELVIS HEAT UP OH WHAT A FINE THING IS A BOY

YES BOYS ARE SO SWEET AND SO AM I OH BOY I'M A DREAM AND NANA SAYS MY DIMPLE IS VERY PRONOUNCED I AM SKIPPING FOR BOYS I AM SKIPPING FOR BOYS I AM DANC-ING LIKE SOMEONE WHO IS PAID TO DANCE FOR BOYS I AM TRIPPING OVER IN FRONT OF THEM I AM BITING MY

TONGUE I AM LIFTING UP MY DRESS I AM BEGGING THE
BOYS TO LET ME COME NEAR I AM KISSING THE BOYS I AM
KISSING THE BOYS THEY ARE KISSING MY BREASTS THEY ARE
KISSING MY BELLY I AM SINKING THROUGH THE MATTRESS
I AM SIGHING I CAN BE HEARD THROUGH WALLS YEAH
BABY OH BABY COS I LOVE TO GET HEARD

2

DYSTOPIAN NOVEL WITH ME AS THE CENTRAL CHARACTER

in the future everyone in the world is depressed ;
it is known as the global downbuzz

in the future   kissing has become lowbrow art
theatre is generously funded
and is performed on outdoor plinths   so high
that no one has to watch
in the future you can have surgery done
to invert your eyeballs   and rig lights on the underside of your skull

in the future   people tell the truth—
they tell it energetically and all the time
it is almost grotesque..........
in the future   during sex   couples scream
the names of other people over and over until climax
then they hold each other and cry

in the future   what youths do at parties is
they just get together and hurt !   wow   like physically
with injuries   new injuries

in the future   at cafés and restaurants
instead of a steady hum of chat   such as we in the present day
are accustomed to   there is a sort of.....grating sound
everyone contributes their own groan
and finds that it builds a sense of community

and where
are the children ?   in the future   they are educating themselves

and each other   they are gathering in town squares
and on the banks of rivers ,   at intersections , on hills ,
under bridges and in the gardens of strangers
and they are just watching...................and making notes

    what else   oh   in the future people embrace the ageing process—
beauty products contain more acid
and in the past in the future   people began a practice
of pulling out their adult teeth at twenty-first birthdays
which they would then gift to city councils   who used the teeth
to build great monuments to peace
   in the future this practice continues but with less anaesthetic
.....as for the monuments :   they have got so tall

   one other thing I know about the future
is that in the future I am dead
   the coroner's report says I buried myself
under one tonne of beanbag beans   and asphyxiated

IF I HAD YOUR BABY IN MY UTERUS I WOULD PROBABLY KILL IT WITH ABORTION

the days are very hard
like dragging myself out of mud with a chain
at least I have a chain   some people are not so lucky
some people   on the other hand   use chains in sex
not you and me though   too much admin
you and me don't even use condoms sometimes
which would shock me if I were fourteen
but I'm not fourteen anymore
I'm a pop sensation and I'm not a little girl anymore
now I'm mean   I wasn't fourteen for very long at all
now I'm this old person in the mud   ah   it's probably good
for my skin   I won't get wrinkles while I wait to die
is that how mud works

you said *periods are cool for me*
cos it means you don't have my baby in your uterus
I was like
if I had your baby in my uterus I would probably kill it with abortion
just like it says in the title okay   it was good the first time I said it
like a soft smack in the face   basically I killed it
—not the baby !   the.....witticism
you looked kind of nonplussed
but only for a moment and then you took it in your stride   said
man that'd be a good title for a collection of poems
you say that about everything   literally everything   it's like all you ever say
and every time   I entertain the idea

don't you ever feel like   uh
everything you and me say is at each other's mercy

that's an imperative   don't ever feel like that
    mirrors facing each other are only interesting because they're facing each other
and honestly I find it infuriating   that I can't catch my own eye
echoing away forever   did I tell you I did a narcissism test on the internet
    I'm so literal baby   nothing is safe
    oh god this is what death feels like   it feels like everything else :
horrible and with no future
    we are just sitting around half-smiling
    I am very quietly whispering to myself :   *cunt.....bitch.....ass*
and you are like   over there in your mud
whispering *man that'd be a good title for a collection of poems*
and dying too   and just hoping the time you're spending with me
is gonna pay off some day

SOMEONE PUTS ON BIZARRE LOVE TRIANGLE
BY NEW ORDER AT A HOUSE PARTY

you have to be half dead to love my god
which isn't like loving normal humans
or normal gods
    if you want to love those kinds of things
they require you to be wholly alive

    I'm half dead and I'm surrounded by the living
    they all walk past   my half-dead ass

    I don't care   god is my husband
and we love each other very much
    I can love my god because I am half-nothing
    I can acknowledge a very large space
    we sit in the dark and we do not touch

    my god shows me my whole life
which is the only theatre I've ever wanted to watch
and every day he drafts my eulogy in his home office

    yeah , my god is dead :
as dead as a white blur in the background of a very old photo ;
as dead as a supermarket trolley in a stream ;
as dead as a roof repairer lying on the ground ;
as dead as a famous painting that someone has kicked a hole in

    I am the only follower of my god
    I always feel embarrassed at the gods parade
carrying my holy text in its plastic spiral binding
    spectators give me pitying looks

but I put my chin up and stamp along like Liesl von Trapp
before she realises she does in fact need a governess

    I sort of wish I were a bit less religious
    every time I pray   I say *can I die for once*
in my life   and every damn time
my god says *not yet*

POOL NOODLE

the air is thick with depression
even the flies   fly very slowly

life is like aqua jogging   but without the flotation device
and the implicit desire to exercise
also it's more the hobby of old men than old women
but old women nonetheless love to get   uhh exclusive about it
e.g. *stop laughing so* loudly *it's not even that funny* ;
crop tops are for girls who are thinner *than you* ;
you have to shave *if you want to wear a dress like that* ;
I don't like girls who scream   et cetera
it's all very manageable and I have no complaints

no one is ever allowed to be mad at me
you can make fun of me though if you want.....
that's my kink
o enable me   and furnish me with false gods
such as full-fat milk ; weed ; and a boyfriend

just let me work myself up for half an hour and I'll be ready—
sexually I mean
look at the water   it's so shiny
I want to dip myself in it
like bread in the hands of a giant ill-mannered French person
life is like aqua jogging in tomato soup :
inexplicable and disgusting
also the tomato soup is actually the menstrual blood
of eleven-year-olds
look at yourself

YOUNG ADULT ROMANCE

yesterday I pulled a very long hair out of the side of my face
and said to George *but it's true   love* is *gonna save us all*

if you choose to be kind to me   I will breathe very loudly in response
I will wake you in the night and force you to join my human pyramid
it is the hazing ritual to which I subject all my new boyfriends
you know exactly and intimately how it works
because you have been my new boyfriend fifteen or twenty times now—
at this point the pyramid is largely a pyramid of you

and if only you had loved me a very little bit
we could have travelled to the Bay of Islands together
to attend what is called Darryl's Dinner Cruise   which is real
perhaps even now   as a gesture   I could take you there blindfolded
in the boot of my car   by which I mean my dad's car
ah , fuck   of the whole pair of us   you're the only one who can drive
we'll have to swap roles for the journey   we'll have to wear wigs
and each other's clothes

perhaps if the joke is big enough you'll recognise me for what I am :
a special treat   for spoilt boys
perhaps then   when I enter the room
you might register a change   the lifting of a miniature weight

all I ask is mild devotion
all I ask is to be taken home via McDonald's   and cradled
while I scream into the massive violent pit of the night

Dad's car got written off and I have never seen your pupils dilate

YOU'VE PUT YOUR EGGSHELL ON THE GROUND , NOW WALK ON IT

I'm sorry for loving you when my love was like a mangled hand
or a suffocating baby   I admit I shouldn't have done that

oh but   not loving you is almost exactly the same as loving you was
in that when I loved you I had to wink all the time   like   all the time
I had to wink constantly to keep you calm
and I thought I might get to stop winking now
(now that there is no ongoing.....tenderness obligation)
but unfortunately I am still winking and I can't seem to stop

it was quite special the way you strained to produce a tear
when you were done breaking up with me   your effort was generous
and your failure endearing   see   I am winking right now
..........or am I ?   that's another wink   or is it
ah   it's okay that you personally   gotta do what you gotta do
it's okay

the pain inside   yeah baby the pain inside
is a hot hot hot hot fire
and I'm always winking   but I'm never even telling a joke

OTHER PEOPLE PEOPLE I HAVE KISSED HAVE KISSED

I have a bad urge
to condescend to a younger woman
there is nothing wrong with her
the wrong thing is with me
the wrong thing is that when I meet her eyes
I want to slice open the skin of my chest in shallow loops
—that's not the wrong part   that's uh normal
—the wrong part is that when I meet her eyes
I try to tell her with my eyes how much I hate myself ,
I try to make her feel like it is her fault

it is not her fault
we have never spoken   the younger woman and I
she has done nothing to me   she is probably gentle
she is probably sweet   probably an okay kisser for a younger woman
but I can't help it   I feel romantic about hating her
I want to scream her name from the rooftops   truly I do—
I want to scream her name and then comprehensively defame it
I want to..........I want to push her into a pool !
I want to push her into a private pool late at night
glowing pale blue in a rich person's back garden   amidst some fucking
palm fronds   I want to push her into a pool so that she screams
and pulls me in with her but in doing so
I want her to accidentally bash my head on the ceramic tiles
and then I just want her to panic in the bloodying water
I want her to find it difficult to breathe   for psychological reasons
while my real breath leaves my real body
in eerie final giggles

I'M SO MENTALLY STRONG IT MOVES ME TO TEARS

have you met me
I'm like an internet video about my own personal hardships
with royalty-free piano music in the background   I'm like a feelings gym
for your married high school friend   mmm   work that empathy

once I left a suicide note for my goldfish
I'm like a goldfish   goldfish have teeth in their throat
I'm like a beautiful rose in a decent man's garden
and a dumbass child has got their skin caught on my thorn
I'm like a house cat   there are no cat flaps and I am glad—
so are the neighbours

once when I was sleepwalking   I committed a murder
once   I ate some glass
once I cut myself in a tender place
when I was trimming my pubes with my weed scissors
once I clawed at my face and hands
then I did it again

I swear I do enjoy my life   I do   dig   my sentience
I enjoy..........spending time
and I am trying to tell myself there are some things
that are worth some.....thing   such as a prize
can I have a prize   I'm serious can I have a prize

sometimes I get feelings and I just can't wait !
to describe them to the therapist my mum pays for
and to get her to say once more that she still
wouldn't think I were evil   if my mum didn't pay her

I would say all this about a fictional character
but why bother   I have this folder in my computer
of selfies I took just before I overdosed
    I think they're cool but I never get to show anyone

BIG HANDSOME BOYS

the final year that I showed up to my old primary school's annual gala ,
I was fifteen and I had a motherfucking boyfriend   that's right cunt
  he played basketball
  we sat in the newest playground with our coolest friends
and discussed my burgeoning inclination to become drunk for the first time

Ursula , our coolest coolest friend—whose red blood cells
have beefed up hard in the intervening years   (and we like to imagine them
doing their macho swagger up and down the veins of her distressingly
beautiful body   her casually alcoholic body
  they are her big handsome boys)
  she was all :   the time is ripe!!!!
let's get this glasses-wearing but also sexually active nerd the fuck off her face
and I was like okay yep

  being fifteen meant my sister was eighteen
which was maybe worth more points even than having a boyfriend
cos she could get us KGBs   which like   if you are old and don't know shit
is a drink you drink when you are fifteen in 2008
  I believe it's named after some kind of   Russian thingy

  well of course I was lovely the first time
and the second time I was still lovely   strolling into the bathroom
to find a girl passed out in the foetal position on the floor
skirt and undies around her ankles   it was the first of my friend's butts
I ever saw   and the third time I knocked Ursula unconscious
by throwing her into a gutter—*I just didn't know my own strength*—
and the fourth time I discovered the urge to jump from great heights
and the fifth time I rediscovered the urge to jump from great heights

but from the third time through the rest of times I have never experienced
an urge as profound as the urge to be rescued
    it's a montage in a coming-of-age film
in which the age is never arrived at   but skidded past ,
course changed laboriously ,   the age skidded past again :
    it's me sprinting away up a Mt Vic street   it's me standing in a garden
in the rain   waiting for my absence to be noticed   me calibrating my face
to achieve a kind of   horny anguish   before I tiptoe out
right through the line of vision of my crush
    me in the corner with a stranger   me pulling off my clothes in the lounge
    me holding a knife and laughing too loudly
    me holding a knife and screaming
    me holding a knife in designer silence
    me swimming away   swimming away out to sea

    it's not a film   it's an eight-year-old getting a ten-minute go
on the PlayStation
at after-school care   pressing buttons randomly
to the sound of boys everywhere groaning and sighing   but not sexily

    my character is largely defined by my need to be rescued—
I mean like in a   post.....post-irony kind of   millennial way though
    it's like   giggling in a cockpit   with big eyes   and jabbing
the big red button and whispering *help* seductively at the co-pilot

    I do my manipulation in the dark   so I can excuse myself after the fact
    this is just a normal human need
to be rescued and then sat with quietly   by some ordinary boy—
to be told things that are not profound   but pretending to be moved
nonetheless   just to get a kiss   just one fucking kiss
    how can I convince you I need you   if I am without a crisis
    there can be no attention given , none received
    I am an eight-year-old in an indifferent adult crowd

that will only turn towards me if I provide a signed statement :
I promise promise promise I am a danger to myself and others

LOSER

I was looking at the stars and I got horny for you
I dunno if the two things were related ;
anyway I stopped looking at the stars out of   um self-respect

how many times
did I wake earlier than I meant to   and roll over
wanting to tell you something ordinary like :
I've just had a dream about you   in which I told you I loved you
and you turned into my ex-boyfriend
and then you turned into T.J. Miller and we had sex—
only to find that you were gone   like Donkey Kong
were you pissing in the garden   no

how many times
did I ask the impression you left in the air
if you were still there

NO ONE WILL EVER BE YOUR BUD IF YOU ARE
NOT YOUR OWN BUD

    we have sent our beloved subjects
out into the wilderness   to go questing for soft drugs
    we have waved them off from the balcony of our luxe house
with lace-edged handkerchiefs

    now   with tired arms   we adjourn to the salon
where we lounge on fur throws   o give me a grape
    there are massive diamonds at our throats
    they are close to drawing blood   which feels nice

    no   we are annoying and white   all our furniture
is painted onto the walls and floors like a bad dollhouse
    we like it like that   (we think we are the winkers   not the winked at)
    we keep dream journals   no we do not

    o we are so depressed   it is almost attractive
    remember when we were skinny   we miss that—
no no—we are faithfully advertising our ease   at the ease convention
and at private home visits   we are the Avon ladies of ease

    we are such good feminists   we keep our apologies to ourselves
    we are crying in the offices of our lady teachers
    it is so charming the way we think we are still in high school
at twenty-three   that is not our age   we're twenty-seven

    we're thirty-two   reading old tweets and sobbing   with all our heads
tucked between our one boyfriend's legs   he can manspread
    we can only come   by imagining ourselves coming
by imagining watching ourselves coming

we're forty-four   cracking open home-insemination kits
that we got from the shop on the cheap
    life continues to be appropriate
    everything in our flat is broken but still working

    we've had a decorative whirlpool installed in the yard
    our friend Eleanor has come over in her slippers
    she is watching us calmly and rolling a joint
while we try out drowning   in our roundabout way

WIDE GARDEN

people call me up sometimes when they wanna die
but other times they forget to call me up   and then they die
   sometimes they don't forget to call me up   but they die anyway
   sometimes
calling me up doesn't even come into it

   my sister walks briskly past intensive care   we are not going there today
   I was there on a different day
sprawled across the carpeted hospital thoroughfare
eating sandwiches   with obligatory slowness
   sandwiches are a death food

   death is a pervert   but I'm a pervert too
   it's crass to chew and breathe like this   given the certainty of death
   I hate it when people say   so-and-so *passed away*
   you wouldn't say so-and-so *passed wind*   you wouldn't say so-and-so's
in the   fucking   *family way*   you wouldn't   you know   steal a handbag
but death makes little sissies of us all

   the landlord knocked down the shed in Jake's garden
and now   the garden is very wide
   we sit in it like   smaller things than we are   there are tears on Jake's face
   I can tell even though it's dark
   I am saying things that are true   I'm saying call me up   I'll answer
but the garden is so wide   it's so wide now

   ah   death   it is as general   as physical junk mail
   imagine going to all the effort of not killing yourself
and then dying anyway   the other day I passed a lady driving a van
   she was pulled up at a red light and she was just screaming
   she was just screaming and screaming

AAAHH!!! REAL DEPRESSION

you know that feeling..........

when.....you've just given birth   to an abomination ?
and then the midwife hands it to you like
you're supposed to love it and   fuckin , clean it   for the rest of time ?

a gross baby has slunk out of me ! I've had such a shock :
it is my depression   god   it is so fugly   I can't even look at it
I get postnatal depression from birthing my first depression
now I got two depressions on my hands and counting
old people shake their heads and glare at me in the street
I don't even know how to masturbate yet..........

look   in this backward country I was not allowed to abort my depression
okay   they were like it'll be both character-building
and um very hip in ten years   just don't tell anyone we said it

but oh what a resilient girl I am—
how clever and resourceful , how unfazed by my   little predicament :
I am in my bedroom wrapping my depressions in cellophane   I am
carrying them around an all-girls high school like a cheap bouquet
so all the girls think it is my birthday   hah
every single day they notice me   (which I love—
I love to be noticed   I love to be noticed by high schoolers)
and they do not pause to question how I can have been born
every single day   of the year

no   I was naturally born—
born to make my way in the world—
I came out of the womb with a bindle over my shoulder
I reckon I am impressive at a young age—

my CV on LinkedIn runs to forty pages ; the list
of awards and scholarships   is very   very long
    I reckon the panel of recruiters will marvel at my wealth of experience
but one or two of them have their doubts :
Kevin's like *um if you've had this many depressions*
how can you still be   you know.....alive

    someone points to my nicely formatted   but functionally insubstantial
History of Suicide   and goes   *have you ever even   like passed out*
    it is at this point that I realise I am not young but fucking old
    the three recruiters are so fresh and sexy..........   *hang on*
I think to myself   *there is a certain fugliness behind all that sex appeal*
that I think I recognise   and then I have it :
I'm being interviewed by three of my own   grown-up depressions
    they have aged well but not too much   like a mid-range cheddar
    I experience a   disconcerting mixture of pride and humiliation
like a good but not award-winning actor in a movie
    we hug and they nepotise me right away

    I shoot up the ranks in a few short years
    Kevin raises his eyebrows and calls me unscrupulous
        god I hate Kevin   I sit in my big office hating Kevin
but not the others   and think to myself   *I am not satisfied*..........
    well if I know anything about capitalism
I mean depression   it's that I personally can have what I want
if I want it enough   and what I want is a large parade—
a large parade to parade my depression around the city
    that'll show Kevin

    boy oh boy do people love to make it easy for me—
I only have to whimper   and they're like *call the friggin mayor*
and it's happening   it's really happening for me
    I mean it's not just for me :

59

it is for everyone to enjoy !!!   I boom through the loudspeakers
spreading my arms like a depressed eagle   I don't feel very IRL
but I do feel.....something
    afterwards   I go around each person on my float
and personally request a pat on the back..........I am   a diva

    I am at a primary-school assembly   telling the children
about my depression   I am saying :
you will probably be depressed when you are older.....
if you are not already depressed
    parents complain   and I do not get paid
for talking about my depression

THIN AIR

amid a great stillness I am thinking my thoughts . no the barb protruding from my stomach does not worry me . no my dispersing parts do not worry me . I simply clench my other parts . I may be unlooked-for . I may be filled with blood . I may grasp a piece of ice if I can find it . I can be amid a stillness but I cannot count myself among it

alone in Room 3 I am papier-mâchéing every surface . I have been papier-mâchéing every surface in Room 3 for twenty-one years . the walls and floor and all the tables and chairs have been thickening . the walls and floor and all the tables and chairs have become thickened and inflamed like an asthmatic airway . I am saving up my breaths to breathe later . I will breathe them later . I will breathe them later when I have survived

AM I ORIGINAL (YEAH) AM I THE ONLY ONE (YEAH)

I COME INTO MY OWN IN A DIMLY LIT ROOM I COME FORTH LIKE A VISITATION UPON MYSELF I COME TO REALISE THAT IF IT WERE EVER POSSIBLE IF IT WERE EVER REMOTELY ACHIEVABLE FOR ME TO COMMUNICATE ABSOLUTELY EVERY SINGLE THING I KNOW AND THINK AND BELIEVE TO ANY OTHER GIVEN PERSON THEN THAT PERSON WOULD CHOOSE TO DIE WOULD CHOOSE TO DIE UNDENIABLY I AM A PROPHET I AM A VISIONARY I AM AN ICON I AM I AM I AM GOD

THREE YEARS AGO I WENT TO SEE A THERAPIST EVERY FORTNIGHT AND EVERY FORTNIGHT I PROMISED HER I WOULDN'T SUICIDE IN THE NEXT FORTNIGHT AND I KEPT MY PROMISES BECAUSE I USED TO KEEP PROMISES I USED TO BE A GOOD GIRL OR AT LEAST I USED TO DO A CREATIVE INTERPRETATION OF THE RIGHT THING MUM SAID ITS OBVIOUSLY THE WORK OF A VERY DISTURBED MIND AND I LAUGHED AND LAUGHED OH HOW I LAUGHED I LAUGHED JUST AS MUCH AS I EVER LAUGH CHRIS SAID THE OBSESSION WITH MORTALITY IN ONE SO YOUNG WAS CONCERNING I FELT PROUD I FELT PROUD I FELT LIKE A PRODIGY A DEATH PRODIGY WHERE AM I NOW

I MUST BLOODLET MY SECRETS I MUST ATTACH PEOPLE TO MY BODY LIKE LEECHES I AM FATTENING THEM UP I AM FORCE-FEEDING MY FRIENDS I AM FORCE-FEEDING MY FAMILY I AM FORCE-FEEDING POTENTIAL EMPLOYERS FOR PERSONAL GAIN BUT I DO IT IN DISGUISE I SAY IT WITH MY MOUTH FULL I SPEAK IT IN TONGUES I TELL IT BUT I TELL

IT SING-SONG LIKE A LULLABY I THINK ABOUT CHILDREN AND I TELL IT MEANER I GO BEHIND A CURTAIN TO SHOW HOW BAD I CAN BE I GO BEHIND A BLACKOUT CURTAIN TO SHOW IT HARDER I SHOW WHAT CAN BE USED TO BURN THROUGH THE THIN SKIN BETWEEN THE IMAGINED SOUL AND THAT OLD DRUMBEAT THAT GOES DIE DIE DIE DIE DIE DIE DIE OH HELL WHAT A CATCHY TUNE OH HELL YOU GOTTA TAP YOUR FEET OH HELL DOESN'T IT MAKE YOU WANNA DANCE

3

PARIS IS ISOLATED FROM THE SEA

once I ate a hard-boiled egg in the gardens of Versailles

it was winter when the trees were bare
and the topiary   concealed under tarpaulins
like foetuses

you have to peel the shell off   which is marvellous

my host family had to teach me a lot of synonyms for *merveilleux*
I used to radiate enthusiasm   back when I was young
the days were harsh and bright   and I took my place among them
wearing a tiara and a backstage pass on a lanyard
holding a champagne flute and charming all the young men
with my tinkling laugh   and sharp nearly-white teeth

a hard-boiled egg is like a boob job   or a suicide   unusual
but understandable

DOUBLE RAINBOW

babies have been conceived and carried to term and born
in the time it has taken me to   comprehensively prove
your inability to grow old with me , baby

I am still young   as young as new hills
and there are so many hearts to break
I'll never fucking get through them all

but at least luck is on my side
by which I mean to say   who *wouldn't* love me
who in this massive world
wouldn't wanna be my especial boyfriend

you and me   have carried out numerous
bolder and paler goes at closeness
it is a traditional dance of hoodwinking
passed down through the ages from asshole to asshole
along with the secret knowledge that rainbows
are actually ovals or something   looked at from above
and that a person   is never actually a good enough person
the audience laps it up and we do too

you and me is like :
there are two people shouting into a massive underground cave system—
one at each end—who are not within earshot of each other
but whose echoes   are within earshot of each other's echoes
you and me   wake in the dark at the same moment

you and me are in a slow-motion replay of a slow-motion replay
that's why it feels like we know the future

BUSINESS

please be advised uhh ..... my body is booming like business ....
I have got a heart but it's beating in a building on the other side of the
city .... my blood however ..... is somewhere accessible only by
manhole ..... the manhole people are all like what the fuck is this ..... what
the fuck is this sluicing off my hi-vis .... I uhh see no need to
disclose the location of my brain at this time ..... it is both uncouth and
irrelevant ..... but my thoughts are like ..... taking place in the half-square-
metre above my head ..... if I stand still they are pretty much in line with
me vertically but if I move around ..... they create a drag on my body that
makes me want to uhh ..... pull my skin off like orange rind .... in
conclusion ..... it is no one's fault but I wish ..... to be abandoned at a roadside
at the edge of a great desert plain ..... and I require help to achieve this

TIMELESS CLASSIC OF CHILDREN'S LITERATURE

when I was a child I visited a farm once
   I was invited to stick my thumb
in one of the long cups   that sucks the udders
   it hurt in a new way   I widened my eyes !

   now that I am grown
I hope the people who surround me on all sides
stroking my arms and hair—
I hope they feel sick   with bad pleasure

   I want to be loved by someone who is doing it
purely to fulfil a self-destructive impulse

   I recall that my thumb came out
feeling like a phantom limb that was still there
   it made me frown in a crafty way like a man—
a man reading his poem aloud   or a man
trying to teach me a lesson

   I felt worried for the cows in an unspecific way
but the farmer said it was good for them

PACK MY ASS FULL OF WEED , LIGHT IT AND SMOKE IT THROUGH MY MOUTH

my name is animal animal .... I live in a mouth-shaped house .... I think about new things every day .... I dig graves but I don't have any corpses to put in them .... I grab hanks of hair in my dreams and wake up with my fists clenched .... in my garden I only grow extremely tiny flowers .... I create a special doll every year to commemorate the dolls I created before ..... then I burn it .... I dream of going to a pitch black space and counting the things I can feel .... once when I was in a widely celebrated restaurant I found the entrance to a hidden room .... inside the hidden room I found the entrance to another hidden room .... I can run faster than everyone I know .... I can appreciate the feeling of an insect on my hand .... the way I move my body is so astonishing .... the green in my eyes appeared after a terrible accident in my childhood .... the air never runs out for me wherever I go .... I go to the carwash every day ..... I observe the cars as they go through the carwash .... the mothers and fathers of others have never enjoyed my presence .... once I traced my index finger down the centre of my abdomen ..... once I dug my knuckles into my neck .... I have a parcel of stones delivered each week for me to redistribute around the countryside .... in my life I have been told many important secrets .... I know there is something special about me because I have heard people say so .... I have been invited to my own surprise party by accident ..... I am waiting in the dark with a large group of people to surprise myself

HERON

saw a heron . while I was seeing the heron I was already wishing I could see the heron again

saw a rat in my skylight . from underneath . the wind was starting to blow around like it remembered itself . I saw that rat a lot over the following days

dogs kept arriving on the property . one was a bulldog . I thought it was a lady by its nipples but it turned out that didn't mean it was a lady . two other dogs came and I took them back to what I thought might be their house . I shut them in there so I hope it was their house

I thought the rat was dying from poison . it was curled up face-down in the skylight . it was holding on to its tail . I thought ' I had better stay here with the rat ..... the rat should have company in its last moments ' . I cried but it was taking too long to die so I went away

finally touched the ginger cat . I don't even like the ginger cat . it distresses me that given the opportunity I touched it anyway

when I came back I expected to see the rat lying very still ..... with stopped breath . instead I saw that it had gone . in the night time I woke to see it in the skylight again . it was eating my ceiling

the heron ..... the heron was so nice to look at . I felt calm to look at it . but I only saw it once

saw a blowfly in my skylight . did not see the rat again

seem to have made friends with the ginger cat . its eyes are so far apart . that is something I never would have known otherwise

NATURE WALK

this mall is huge .... it's like that Joni Mitchell song except that I care less .... it's like when Counting Crows covered that Joni Mitchell song .... I'm walking through this huge mall in an unclean skirt and a white T-shirt .... the white T-shirt has been washed but it is still yellow in the armpits .... my sister says I dress how I do specifically to piss her off .... when I was a child I wanted to be a motivational speaker .... I am bad at games like Werewolf unless I am one of the werewolves .... if I am a werewolf I just play how I would if I were a villager cos I feel guilty about being a werewolf ..... it feels less evil to act like a villager ..... for some reason this works if you are a werewolf but not if you are a villager .... I guess I am a pretty good werewolf .... if you sacrifice the other werewolves you can convince people that you are a villager ..... then you can be the best werewolf and also the werewolves ultimately win .... I try to do nice things in secret and then I tell people that I have tried to do nice things in secret .... Ursula says that my self-disgust is so performative it's self-defeating ..... like I'm so self-aware that my self-awareness becomes wrong .... I'm so aware that my self-awareness is wrong that my self-awareness becomes right .... it's Mental Health Awareness Week .... this mall is huge .... underneath my clothes I am wearing baggy undies and a push-up bra .... I can feel the baggy undies falling down ..... but I am doing a good job of pretending that I can't

ORDINARY DAY BY VANESSA CARLTON AUTOPLAYS WHILE YOU ARE BONING

baby you take some liberties   look at you
emerging through elevator doors in a tuxedo
and striding into my hot yoga studio   in the middle of a class

you are riding a near-empty train with a pot plant—
and catching my eye from the other end of the carriage
and then catching eye again
    I am riding in a hot air balloon—
we are looking at each other through binoculars
    you are taking me to your high school reunion
having convinced me it's fancy dress   and I have arrived covered in fake blood
    I have transformed into a smooth stone
and you are painting a pink heart on me
with a yellow background   and presenting me to your mum on Mother's Day
    we are in an awesome movie   sighing in separate beds—
the images are overlaid so it looks like we're in the same bed

look I actually think you are so..........great—
it makes me wanna investigate your neck for signs of a full-head silicon mask ;
it makes me wanna cast your face in plaster and post it to the future ;
it makes me wanna boogie ! like a spooked horse

okay baby okay   it's true that I only ever tell the truth sideways
whereas the first thing you said the third time we met
was   *you're real*   and it catapulted me back in time
to sixth-form English   final period on a Thursday—
the bell ringing and ringing—my face on the desk—
my heart suddenly unfamiliar—my brain snagged painfully on the future—
my body panicking   at the unthinkable thought
of having to wait ten years for you

LOOK ME IN THE ASS AND TELL ME THAT YOU'RE HAPPY NOW

I liked our hi-tech science laboratory , baby !

you used to invent for me a sex in which
I would faint over and over in a ballroom
with pretty glass baubles hanging from the ceiling
or—not faint over and over exactly   but rather travel back in time
every few seconds   to faint the same faint with renewed gusto
so like   time   and time again

I on the other hand
used to try to invent for you a sex in which
the ultimate goal was to get you to finally learn how to love
    yours was ultimately more original and more poignant—
you always said mine was too on the nose   laughing
as you approached climax

I didn't mind because of the large windows
that I could turn and look out of

but that damn laboratory ! just got burned to the ground in a
freak accident   we are standing in the ruin when you turn to me
and say *I think this is the right time to tell you I want a divorce*

well I reply :
I am   not surprised by this , baby
    I want to sound sexy and mystical and also touchingly gracious
but it comes out like a dubbed animal in a TV movie
    I turn to look out a window but of course the walls
have burnt right down   and the frames just open out onto the sky

ugh..........real life is so obvious
we are agreeing about this as if we are in love
when suddenly   we have a terrible thought at the same moment :
oh god   what about the dogs—
what about our two prize Italian Greyhounds

.... !

'oh ha ha it's fine   we got them in the future it's cool
oh ! we're still young   phewf

I DM you a stock image of someone throwing a shaka   and I go home
without crying   I can do this because I've spent my whole life
doing kegels   but for my eyes..........and I'm just too strong
I look in the mirror and practise my self-affirmations :
hey ! you are both interesting and generous
which you worked hard on okay   you worked hard and you deserve the pay-off

yeah I am like I earned my millions flipping houses
but instead of houses it was people   I always make sure I get out
a little more than I put in   so I have more to offer the next one
and that entitles me to love , bitch
if you won't love me I'll have to do some like..........creative accounting

ONE LESS PLACE I CAN PUT MY DICK INTO

it's not like no one's ever referred to their dick as vitamin D before
but it worked embarrassingly well on me
like mmm yeah alleviate my depression baby
give me that simple solution :
exercise   sleep   ....Brazil nuts   and dick

you are so kind   the way you accepted me for who I am
like *you can kinda pull off mouth herpes   it kinda fits your aesthetic*
and you are so clever   to have thought of sticking a kick me sign
on my back   when we were kissing
and you are so good at jokes   like when I said *I love you*
and you said *I love scratching my big balls*

and aren't I so.....   aren't I so um , ungenerous—   yeah ha ha plot twist :
you're actually not the villain—it's just   so easy to paint you
in a really bad light   like so people can literally barely see you
sorry baby   what else can I do

really our narrative has been tolerable !   almost charming—
like..........the past   or a primary-school rock band
and I wish everyone knew the diverse ways in which you saved my ass
I tell you I'm trying to undo everything I ever said about you
in one breath , and you laugh
and ask if I can attach a handsome photo of you too

I wish I had the stranglehold on language that I pretend to have
but my mother tongue is a massive museum of failures to express love
and I'm just on a class trip making sketches for high school art
language laughs at me , not the other way around
so there is no beautiful way to tell you how beautiful you made me
while I was attempting to   curb-stomp your.....   emotional availability

I wanted much more than what you could give
　　you thought it was love　what you weren't managing to do
because that's what I told you
but in fact it was hate　it was hate that I wanted :　thick , luxe hate—
the kind you can only do to someone who means everything to you ,
which is to say　the kind only I can do to myself
and I'm sorry baby　you couldn't help

KNICKERS

the house next door burns down for something to do .... it is so intriguing ..... like finding out you have a twin ..... or being able to communicate verbally with animals .... we climb in through a window frame ..... there isn't any glass ..... and land in a clawfoot bath .... my boyfriend gives me a set of lingerie ..... which is a weird thing to receive on my fifth birthday .... I get a new boyfriend ..... sweet Harry .... it is true love .... we kiss on the mat and he gives me a locket .... isn't that nice .... I never put anything in it .... my parents divorce so we have to break up

a firefighter breaks the neighbourhood swing .... I think : shouldn't they fix it .... my sister rearranges the furniture in our bedroom again .... Dad does my plaits .... Mum gets a flat on the Terrace and buys us bunks .... she sits on the floor and reads us books ..... for example Helen Keller but the final page is missing .... don't read anything into that ..... it's just something that happens .... I stand in the garden with my arms held out like branches for several minutes .... not a single bird takes me up on it ..... the bastards .... I slam my bedroom door so hard that it comes off its rollers and falls through the room .... I am angry when I am eight ..... I get docile later

when I am nine the man next door has a very long beard .... he lives with his old mother and she believes in god .... we stand in the kitchen and listen to him yell ..... watch him arrange the air around his head with his hands ..... just so ..... watch him wrench it apart again .... my sister shuts the attic door while I am still up there .... I was asking for it .... I mean I literally asked her to do it .... hmm ..... I never know if I'm six or if I'm twenty-six and talking to my therapist .... either the past or the present is very easy to visit .... the difference is in one of them everyone calls underpants *knickers*

REASONABLE REQUESTS

I want you to poison me slowly
in order specifically to flirt with me on my deathbed

I want to perform for you a striptease
to music being played in your flatmate's bedroom

I want you to look at me
backwards through a telescope   and exclaim
' huh.....how small '

I want you to draw me without looking at the paper
and turn out to have drawn someone else

I want you to drag a person from the sea out of moral duty
and have that person turn out to be me

I want you to forget to turn your phone off at my funeral
but for it not to ring anyway

I want you to say to me *there's probably a parallel universe in which I love you*

I want you to love me as an elaborate prank
that you carry out purely for your own entertainment

I want to loiter in your presence so quietly
that you remain   entirely undisturbed

I want to be at the top of the list of things you are indifferent to
and I want you to be at the top of the list of things that are indifferent to me

I want my face on the front page of a newspaper
on display in a shop window

in the background   of a single panel in a critically acclaimed graphic novel

that comes out when I'm thirty   or already dead
I want you to get it out of the library and skim-read it

NO ONE OWNS ME LESS THAN YOU

I could love you better   I know I could
that's what I told myself   according to the history books—
and I can confirm it because..........I was there
    what a privilege to have been in my head
and to have witnessed such momentous events

    such as the day I opened my eyes underwater
and saw what must have been your hands
and then closed my eyes again..........
and such as every single other day
    I spent each one thinking only about my own hands
and wanting to scrub them very hard
and line my fingers up in front of you like the seven dwarves
but.....ten of them   and you're Snow White and you're like *ayayai*

    I thought *one day I will become as pure as a blood donation*
and that is the day we will have our baby
    that way I could have held her and kissed her little baby head
    she would have been our baby and we would have cried
but beautiful crying like all soft light
and thin linen curtains in a gentle breeze
    the hair on our heads would've been really lush
and we'd've had no other hair on our bodies
    we'd've been taking fucking nineties family portraits with our baby

    I'm   uh definitely sadder about aborting that fake one
than I would be about aborting a foetus in this version of reality
    I'm not actually allowed babies here anyway
    I like to imagine somewhere I could love and be loved by you
and we could like   put our arms around each other
and you could push back my hair   yeah   like in a porno for tender ladies

and kiss my temple   it would be easy
cos my temple is very..........spacious   baby it'd be hard to miss
     people would see you doing this and think :
neither of them can ever possibly have treated the other badly
and neither of us   and none of our
what are they called   future ancestors
none of our   oh—descendants—
none of them would ever suicide

ALL YOU PEOPLE CAN'T YOU SEE CAN'T YOU SEE HOW YOUR LOVE'S AFFECTING OUR REALITY

I LOVE TO FEEL THIS WAY I LOVE TO FEEL THIS MEDIUM WAY I LOVE TO HAVE BECOME ESTRANGED FROM MY MENACE TO HAVE BROKEN MY VOWS TO MY MENACE TO HAVE MADE A CHOICE THIS IS A CHOICE THIS IS NOT A RANDOM TRICKLE FROM ONE SECTION OF TIME TO THE NEXT THIS IS A NEW FRONTIER THIS IS SPACE TRAVEL AND I'M SO GRATEFUL FOR THE HELMET I'M SO GRATEFUL FOR THE SUIT I'M SO GRATEFUL FOR THE STEADY SUPPLY OF OXYGEN AND THAT MY FACE IS NO LONGER PRESSED INTO THE EARTH BUT I CAN'T DENY I FIND MYSELF A LITTLE DISTURBED BY ALL THE OTHER FLOATING BODIES POPULATING MY NEWLY SWOLLEN FIELD OF VISION

BUT THERE IS A BLINDNESS TOO THERE IS A FEELING OF BLINDNESS THERE IS A FEELING OF FEELING MY WAY BACKWARD AROUND A ROOM IN THE DARK A ROOM IN A LARGE HOUSE IN A DIFFERENT CITY I KEEP GETTING BRUISES HUGE BRUISES I KEEP FALLING OVER I KEEP GETTING A SURPRISE BUT NOT THE SURPRISE I WANT I WANT A NEW KIND OF PAIN SO I STOP EATING JUST TO KEEP A LITTLE VIOLENCE ALIVE I SENSE A WEIRDNESS PRICKING AT ME BUT I TALK OVER IT I TALK AND TALK I LOVE TO SIT IN A CHAIR I LOVE TO WIDEN MY STANCE I LOVE TO PUT MY HAND ON MY KNEE AND HOLD FORTH

I CAN NEVER TELL ENOUGH OF THE TRUTH THE TRUTH JUST KEEPS GETTING FASTER LIKE A CAR FILLED WITH CRIMINALS I'M THE MAN CHASING IT BUT I'M OUT OF SHAPE I HAVE TO SLOW TO A STOP BEFORE I EXPECT TO

HAVE TO SLOW TO A STOP I HAVE TO BEND OVER TO DRY
RETCH AS THE TAIL LIGHTS ROUND A CORNER AND I
KNOW I HAVE LET EVERYONE DOWN BOY HAVE I BEEN A
LET-DOWN I HAVE DROPPED MY SELF DOWN INTO A VERY
DEEP WELL AND I AM STANDING AT THE TOP STARING IN
LIKE A PSYCHOPATHIC CHILD I AM WATCHING MY SELF
FALLING DOWN DOWN DOWN THE SCREAMS GETTING
FAINTER BUT UP HERE I AM JUST WATCHING AND THERE
IS A SMALL SMILE PLAYING ABOUT MY LIPS

TURDUCKEN

I blow my body around like   the huge clump of brown hair
that I once saw blowing up Cuba Street
    I follow its movements with interest
    I put a video of it on the internet

    my favourite brag
is that a groundskeeper once told me I was the whole package—
good bants good body he said
    he also said I was a piece of ass   and then apologised immediately—
said he'd never called anyone that before   put his head in his hands

    I use up my body like bait   I keep my body in a bucket
    I keep a bucket by my bed
    once after boning a drug dealer   the drug dealer asked me
to read him a bedtime story   I read him the whole of *The Velveteen Rabbit*
then he thanked me kindly and went to sleep

    I remember everything—
it's one of my bad habits

    I remember a nurse once tried to convert me
to Christianity in a hospital bathroom
just after I'd done a shit...................job   of trying to kill myself
    at first I misheard her   I thought she said the thing that saved her life
was *finding gold*   I laughed and laughed in her arms
then I stopped and said   *wait*

    I'm much better at suicide jokes than I am at dying
and I'm not even that good at suicide jokes   so I may be immortal
    my jokes are very cheap   just like me
but I can't help it—I'm on the benefit—the sickness benefit

my sense of humour is in itself   a sickness benefit   it is my right

I suppose I'm a new bigot   in that I spread hate—
but the hate that I spread is bespoke—
it's artisanal baby   bad poetry is my small business
with the brand statement : *a little self-loathing goes a long way*   like
don't go for a jog   do not do a face mask   don't take a bath

I put my body in a bath once
I sat in the bath and ate a bag of Twisties
the Twisties were orange   which is normal for Twisties
the bathwater was also orange   which is not normal for bathwater
but I had used an orange bath bomb   which was a way of pushing the boat out
my body is a boat   no
my body is a car in the sea with a drowned thing inside
and they talk about bodies of water
and they talk about the body of a car
my body is a car in the sea with a drowned thing inside
my body's in a body and a body's in me
do I need to say it....................turducken
no   I did not need to say it
my body is a car with a drowned thing inside
pulled up and away from the sucking sea floor by a crane
my body is unswallowed and dangling above the water
dripping orange drips

I remember everything
but my body always tells it wrong
which is a terrible betrayal :
the nurse said I was lying when I said she had tried
to sell god to me in the bathroom
I wasn't
but my body was too tired to convince anyone

ACKNOWLEDGEMENTS

Lots of people have helped me write this book. Help has come in many forms over several years, and I owe huge thanks to everyone who has read my poems, given me advice, made me think new things, made me laugh, made me dinner, made my bed, made me ask questions, coaxed me out of myself, let me stand on a stage, challenged me, encouraged me, roasted me, given me a kiss, listened to me, forgiven me, kept me alive, or some nuts combination of the above.

For those reasons and more I wish especially to say: thank you Ursula, without whom these poems would be much, much stupider, as would I. Thank you Eamonn for your excellent company and unwavering support. Thanks Callum for the cover, no one else could've. Thank you so much Ashleigh, Fergus, Therese, Kirsten and VUP, I feel exceptionally lucky to have you on my team. Thank you Hera for like . . . believing in me. Thank you TMI. Thanks NYWF. Thank you Uther. Thank you Chris and the MA class of 2014. Thanks James and the CREW253 class of 2013. Thanks Dan, thank you PlayShop. Thank you Long Cloud, thanks Stella, Aaron, Sophie, Jo, Leo Gene, Aileen. Willem, you gave me the world, I wish I could thank you. Thanks Mr Watson-Jones, you're very important. Thanks JD and WGC, sorry about the title, and about the c-word. Thanks Show Ponies, you're so sexy. Thanks Oli, you're a genius. Thanks Eleanor for Fridays. Thanks Ox and Eddie, my two dads. Thanks Jakey baby. Thanks Kezia, you're a real brick. Thank you Patar, Livvy, Lizzy, Paddy, Ella, Ella, George, Ang, Eleanor, Hannah, Alex, Ellie, Louise, Fi, Julian, Timmy, Mish and Ayrton; each of you has on at least one occasion helped to pull me out of somewhere very dark and lonely and I'm deeply grateful to have had the pleasure of living with you. Thanks Laura for hugging me at that party. Thank you Peter for being kind. Thank you Penny, you are a fish. Thank you to my therapist. Thanks EMDR. Thanks Shrek, thanks Outkast, thanks the Backstreet Boys, thanks New Order, thanks that *Wonder Woman* movie, thanks Vanessa Carlton. Thanks Briscoes, thanks

McDonald's. Thanks Ebony, thanks Carlucci Land. Finnius . . . 'thanks'. Thank you to my big, warm, funny, sharp, ridiculous, generous family, I'm so stoked to be among you. And thank you Mum, thank you Dad, thank you Elise, sorry I'm like this, thank you for loving me anyway, I love you all very very much.

* * *

Some of these poems have previously appeared in other publications, including *Confetti*, *Going Down Swinging*, *Mimicry*, *Minarets*, *Scum Mag*, *Shabby Doll House*, *Sick Leave*, *The Spinoff*, *Sport*, *Strays* by Foundlings Press, *Sweet Mammalian* and *Tell Me Like You Mean It*. Thank you for having me.